DATE DUE			
MAY 9			
JUL 5 '79			
WAY 1 3 '93			
NOV 2 1993			
NOV 2 9 1993			
NOV 2 8 1995			
APR 2 7 1999			
MAY 0 5 2000			
APR 2 6 2006			
MAR 1 9 2008			
APR 1 3 2011			
MAY 1 3 2011			

IDEAL 3370 UNGUMMED, 3371 GUMMED   PRINTED IN U.S.A.

ABOUT THE BOOK

Many hundreds of year ago, Indians lived in part of Central America and Mexico. One group of Indians were called the Maya. They built beautiful stone temples and large cities.

They developed a writing system.

They made paper and wrote books.

They invented a remarkable number system.

They studied astronomy and made an accurate calendar.

They used rubber for shoes and made rubber balls.

They made several kinds of musical instruments.

This book tells you about some of the wonderful things that the Maya knew and did so long ago. It also tells you how to perform experiments so that you can do some things the Maya did. While having fun you can see how these useful, scientific ideas work in action.

You will enjoy the dramatic and interesting pictures, which show the daily life of the Maya.

THE MAYA KNEW

THE MAYA KNEW

by
TILLIE S. PINE
and
JOSEPH LEVINE

**PICTURES BY
ANN GRIFALCONI**

McGRAW-HILL BOOK COMPANY
New York · St. Louis · San Francisco · Düsseldorf · Johannesburg
Kuala Lumpur · London · Mexico · Montreal · New Delhi · Panama
Rio de Janeiro · Singapore · Sydney · Toronto

Over fifteen hundred years ago, long, long
before the Spanish explorers came to the New World,
there were people living in Central America,
in Yucatan and in other parts of Mexico.
These people were the Maya.

Many of the people who live in these places
today are descended from the early Maya.
Scientists say that the Maya were the only people in the
New World to develop an original writing system,
to make paper from trees and use this paper to make books.
They also made and used rubber.
They even invented a remarkable number system.

As you read this book, you will find out how the Maya
did these things and other things
so many, many hundreds of years ago.

The Maya knew

how to make paper from the bark
of wild fig trees. Some scientists believe
that they were the only people in the New World to make
paper from bark. The Maya called their paper - - - *huun.*
They stripped the inner bark from the wild
fig trees and soaked it in water to soften it.
They pounded on the softened bark with wooden
beaters. The pounding made the bark
thinner and much wider.
After the bark dried, the Maya cut it into long, wide
strips. They painted both sides of the strips
with ground white limestone mixed with water.
This was their paper.
The Maya used this bark-paper for writing, for drawing,
and even for making some of their clothing.

Today

we make most of our paper
from wood. Lumbermen cut down trees in
forests and send the logs to paper mills. Large
machines grind the logs into tiny pieces. Then workers
mix the pieces with water, starch, glue, and chemicals.
They heat the mixture in huge vats until the mixture
becomes a pulp. They spread the pulp on large screens to
dry and then roll it into flat sheets. This is our paper.

You

can make paper but you will make it from rags.
Pull apart a piece of old linen, the size
of a small handkerchief, until you have
a pile of threads. Cut these threads into tiny pieces
and put them into a small pot. Cover the threads
with water and boil them for 10 minutes. Add half a glass
of liquid starch and boil for 5 minutes more. Lay a small
wire screen on a bowl in the sink. Let the mixture cool
and pour it evenly over the screen. Lift the screen with
the threads on it, put it between 2 dishtowels and roll
a rolling pin over it so that the water is pushed out
of it. Take away the towels. Let the layer
of threads dry overnight, then peel it
carefully from the screen. You have
made paper. Write on it.

The Maya knew

how to make a special kind of book.
They folded their bark-paper
into sections like a folding screen. Each section
was about 5 inches wide and 9 inches long.
They attached stiff boards
to the first and last sections
of the folded paper and decorated the boards.
They wrote across the folded sections from left to right.
Some of their books had as few as eight sections;
other books had as many as twenty-eight sections.
The Maya wrote books about
their history, medicine, astronomy and their gods.

Today

we make many kinds of books.
Authors write about many different things.
These writings are printed on paper
and the pages are bound into books in factories.
We also put decorated covers on our books.

You

can make a book that looks
like a Maya book.
Fold a large sheet of blank paper into 4 sections
like a screen. Cut 2 pieces of cardboard, the same
size as the sections of your folded paper. Paste
a cardboard on each of the outside sections.
Now you are ready to write a story
in your book—after you read
the next two pages.

The Maya knew

how to develop a writing system
by using glyphs (glifs).
Glyphs are pictures of faces, animals and signs
fitted into squares. These glyphs told about
different ideas and events. Some scientists think
that the glyphs also stood for different sounds.
They say that the Maya system used as many
as 492 glyphs. The Maya writing was done
by their priests and their ruling families.
They were the only people in the New World
who had developed an original system of writing
long before the Spanish explorers came.

Today

there are different kinds
of written languages all over
the world. Many people use alphabets.
Our alphabet has 26 letters in it. These
letters stand for different sounds. We use
these letters to make our words and these
words make up our written language.
Other people, like the Chinese, have
written languages that use characters
or signs to tell about ideas and activities.

You

can make up your own signs and pictures
that stand for words and ideas. Make
small signs and pictures that stand for
a sunny day, a mountain range, a river,
a tree, a rock, a house, a boy, a girl.
Write a story across the sections of
your "Maya book" using your signs
and pictures.
Decorate your cover. Ask a friend
to "read" your story.

The Maya knew

how to make a number system

They invented three signs to stand for numbers:

a dot . for 1;   A line ___ for 5,

an egg-shaped sign ⬭ for 0.

The Maya were the first people in the world to use the zero
in a number system.

They wrote the numbers 1 to 19 this way:

.	..	...	....	___	.	..	...	....
1	2	3	4	5	6	7	8	9

=	.	..	...	....		.	..	...	....
10	11	12	13	14	15	16	17	18	19

They had a special way of writing numbers
higher than 19. When they did this, they used the zero
to help them.

You will learn about this way on page 36.
The Maya merchants used their number
system in their business.

The priests used it when they wrote
about their studies.

The Maya also used their number system
to record important dates in their books
and on their carved stones.

Today

we too have a number system.
We use the numbers 0 through 9.
Our written numbers get larger from right to left.
The first column on the right
is the units column—from 0 through 9.
The next column to the left
is the tens column—from 10 through 99.
The next column to the left
is the hundreds column—from 100 through 999.
Each column of numbers is 10 times larger
than the column to its right. In this way we can write
numbers into the millions and billions.
But—we read and write our numbers from left to right.
We call our numbers—Arabic numbers.

You

can do simple arithmetic examples
using the Maya number system.
Find the answers to these examples
and write your answers in Maya numbers:

.... plus ... equals?   ... minus .. equals?

Have fun working out other examples
with Maya numbers.

The Maya knew

how to study the sky to make a calendar.
They built high stone towers, called - - - *caraculs,*
with winding stairways inside. They left
openings in the walls of the room at the top of each tower.
The Maya priests studied the changing
positions of the sun and the stars
through these openings. In this way they learned
that it takes a little more than 365 days
to make one year. They found that it takes
that time for the sun and the stars to be seen again
in the same positions in the sky.
Using these studies of the sky,
the Maya made a calendar of 18 months
of 20 days each and one month of 5 days.
They used their calendar to tell them when to plant
their crops, when to harvest them,
and when to celebrate their festivals.
They also studied the positions of the moon
and found that it takes between 29 and 30 days
from one full moon to the next full moon.
They even learned how to tell when the eclipses
of the sun and the moon would take place.

Today

we have our own calendar. We know that it takes the
Earth one year of 365¼ days to revolve around the sun.
Our year is divided into 12 months.
Every fourth year, one day is added to our year
to make up for the four quarter-days left out of our calendar.
We call that year a leap year.
Any year that can be divided evenly by 4 is a leap year.
You can figure out when we will have the next leap year.

You

can find out for yourself how many days pass from the time
you see a full moon to the next full moon.
Get a calendar and mark the date
when you see the full
round face of the moon. As the days go by,
you see a smaller part of the moon.
Count the number of days that pass until you see
the full round face of the moon again.
You might call this number
of days—a moon-month.

The Maya knew
how to make and use mortar.

They heated limestone in a kiln
until the limestone became a powder.
We call this powder - - - lime. Then they
mixed the lime with gravel and water
until it became a thick paste.
We call this paste - - - mortar.

The Maya used mortar to hold
the stones together when they built
their temples, houses and walls. Sometimes
they used this mortar to plaster
their stone walls.

Today

we mix lime, sand,
water, and plaster of Paris or
cement to make our mortar. We use
this mortar for holding bricks and stones
together in our buildings, walls, and bridges.

You

can make your own mortar.
Buy a small, inexpensive bag
of plaster of Paris in a paint store.
Mix some plaster of Paris with sand
and a little water to make a thick paste.
This is mortar. You can put a thick
coat of mortar on the sides and top of a covered
cardboard box. As you are doing this, put
pebbles and sea-shells into the wet mortar.
Let the mortar dry. Do you see how
firmly the plaster holds the pebbles and
shells in place? Use your decorated
box as a small plant stand.

The Maya knew

how to make their work easier.
More than 3000 years ago, they, like people
in other parts of the world, made
simple tools to help them.
They made hammers of wood and of stone.
They made chisels of stone. They used these tools
to cut and carve stone blocks
for their temples and for their sculpture.
They also used these tools to cut down trees.
The Maya hardened the ends of long, strong
sticks over a fire. They used these sticks
as tools to dig holes in the hard ground
when they planted their corn, beans, squash,
tomatoes and yams.
The Maya also used stones as tools
to grind their corn. They called the grinding
stone a Kab. They put the corn on a flat
stone and ground the corn with the Kab.

Today

we, too, know how to
make our work easier. We make all kinds of
tools to help us. We use steel, wood, and plastic
to make hammers, chisels, saws, screwdrivers,
pliers, and many other tools.
We also make electric tools—saws,
drills, sanders.

You

can make your work easier
by using simple things as tools. Get a narrow,
flat piece of wood 6 inches long.
Cut one end to a point. Sandpaper the long
edges of your wood halfway down from
the point to make these edges sharper.
Use this "tool" as a letter opener.
Use a stone as a hammer
to open some hard-shell nuts.
Wrap these nuts in a dishtowel
and use a soda bottle as a roller
to crush the nuts. You can
sprinkle the crushed nuts
on your pudding.

The Maya knew

how to make rollers and use them to help
move heavy stones more easily.
They split off blocks of limestone from the
mountainsides with their stone chisels,
wooden hammers, and long poles.
They cut down trees and made logs into rollers
from the trunks of these trees.
They pushed and pulled heavy stones
over these log-rollers for long distances
to the places where they used these stones
to build high pyramids, temples and palaces.

Today

we sometimes use large rollers
when we move a small house a short
distance. Some large food stores use roller-slides
to move heavy food baskets to the pick-up stations.
But most of the time we use trucks and trains
on wheels to move heavy weights
from one place to another.

You

can find out how to move things more easily by using
rollers. Place a pile of books on a table. Push slowly.
Now—place 5 round pencils in a row, 3 inches
apart from each other. Put the pile of books
on top of your pencils. Push the books
again. Do the rolling pencils help
you move the books
more easily?

The Maya knew
how to build a straight, flat, raised
road over rough uneven land.
They used stone and mortar to build
the side walls of this raised road.
They filled in the low places between these
walls with gravel and stone. Then the Maya
covered the top of the evened-out road
with white cement. They smoothed
the surface with a huge stone roller that took
15 men to push over the road.
The Maya called this road - - - a *sacbe*.
We call it a causeway.
The Maya built most of their "causeways"
leading to their temples.

Today

we make some of our roads level
by building causeways over low places.
We fill in these low places with stone
and gravel. We pave the roadway
with asphalt or concrete. We roll
the causeways smooth with huge
road-rolling machines.

You

can see different kinds of raised roads.
Next time you go on an automobile trip
look for raised roads on highways.
You may also see raised
road-beds for trains.

The Maya knew

how to make musical sounds
by striking things together and by blowing
into shells and tubes.
They used things they found around them
to make their simple musical instruments.
They blew into large seashells and used them
as trumpets. They used large turtle shells as drums
and deer horns as drumsticks.
They hollowed out logs, covered the ends
with deerskin, and used these, too, as drums.
They shaped clay into tubes and made
finger holes in them. They blew into these tubes
and used them as flutes.
The Maya played their musical instruments
on holidays and festivals.

Today

we make striking instruments - - -
drums, cymbals, triangles,
pianos, xylophones. We call these
percussion (per-kŭsh-en) instruments.
We make blowing instruments - - -
trumpets, flutes, saxophones, clarinets, horns.
We call these wind instruments. We use different materials
to make these instruments—wood, metal, animal skin.

You

can make musical sounds by making
your own percussion and wind instruments.
Put the plastic cover on an empty coffee can and beat
the cover with the eraser end of your pencil. Hit
two metal pot lids together to sound like cymbals.
Make a toy flute of a paper drinking straw.
Flatten one end of the straw. Cut away one inch
on each side of this end to make it pointed.
Make 4 holes, one inch apart, along one side
of the straw. Blow into the pointed end. Make
music by covering different holes with your
fingers as you blow. Use these "instruments"
when you and your friends play together.

The Maya knew

how to carve on stone.
They used their stone chisels and wooden
hammers to do this. They carved figures,
writing, and numbers on slabs of stone
when they wanted to tell the stories
of important events in their lives.
We call these carved stones - - - *stelae*.
The Maya set up their stelae in and around
temples, public buildings, and along their roads.

Today

we carve in stone,
and we use hand tools and electric
tools to do this. We make stone sculpture. We carve words
and figures on the walls of post offices,
libraries, courthouses, and other public buildings.
We also carve sayings on stone monuments and gravestones
in memory of people.

You

can carve a figure on a bar of soap.
Use a pointed nail file as your carving tool.
When you finish the figure, carve out
the date at the bottom of the soap.
You can also look for buildings
and monuments that have carved writings
on their surfaces. Read what these writings say.

The Maya knew

how to make and use rubber.
They found out that certain trees had a special
white liquid in them. They called these trees - - - *Cau-uchu.*
This means "weeping wood."
They made cuts in the bark of the trees and the white
liquid dripped out. We call this liquid - - - *latex.*
The Maya collected the liquid in pots. They dipped
the end of a stick into the liquid and dried it
over a smoky fire. They kept doing this
until layer after layer of rubber formed
on the end of the stick. They took the rubber
off the stick and rolled it into a ball for their games.
They sometimes covered their feet
with the liquid and let it dry on their feet.
The Maya were the first people
to make "rubber shoes."

Today

we take latex from rubber trees
and change it into rubber
by heating and drying the latex. We also
make "man-made" rubber from special
chemicals. We use rubber in making balls,
tires, erasers, clothing, covering for electric
wire, rubber bands, and many other things.

You

can make a small ball from rubber cement.
Put the tips of your fingers into the rubber cement.
Rub your wet fingers together. Your warm fingers
dry the cement and you feel a tiny ball forming.
Dip the tiny ball into the cement.
Roll it and dry it with your fingers,
the same way. Do this a few times.
You now have a small rubber ball.
Bounce your ball.

The Maya knew
how to use a solid rubber ball
in a special game they played.
They called the game - - - *pok-a-tok*.
They built a long narrow court outdoors.
They hung a stone ring on the wall at each end
of the court. The players tied animal skin pads on
their elbows, wrists and hips. They hit the hard rubber ball
with these parts of their bodies, and the ball bounced off.
They were not allowed to use their hands.
The players tried to hit the ball through
the stone ring. It was very hard to do.
The winners often received gifts of jewelry
from the people watching.

Today

we play many kinds of games
and we use balls of different sizes,
shapes, and materials. We play
soccer, football, baseball, basket ball,
tennis, golf, and handball. Most of the balls
used in these games have rubber in them to
make the balls bounce better. In some of the
games, the players wear special uniforms and
equipment to protect themselves from injury.

You

can find out how rubber helps a ball to bounce
better. Make a ball by winding about 5 yards
of cord around a wad of paper. Bounce this ball
on the floor. Unwind the cord. Now wind the
same cord around a small rubber eraser.
Bounce this ball. Which bounces higher?
The one with the rubber inside does,
because the rubber helps it bounce.

THE MAYA NUMBER SYSTEM

On page 16, we promised to show you how the Maya wrote numbers higher than 19.

In their system, the Maya made their numbers larger from bottom to top. They wrote their numbers on what we call "steps." Numbers 1 through 19 were on the first·step. So—on the first step:

a dot · meant 1; a bar—meant 5; a bar and a dot over it—meant 6; three bars and two dots over them ≡ meant 17.

Numbers 20 through 399 needed a second step up. The numbers on this step were 20 times larger than numbers on the first step. So—on the *second* step:

a dot   ·   meant 20 (20 x 1)

a bar — meant 100 (20 x 5)

a bar and a dot over it ∸ meant 120 (20 x 6)

three bars and two dots over them ≡ meant 340 (20 x 17)

Numbers 400 through 7,999 needed a third step up. The numbers on this step were 20 times larger than numbers on the second step. So—on the *third* step:

a dot   ·   meant 400 (20 x 20 x 1)

a bar —— meant 2,000 (20 x 20 x 5)

a bar and a dot over it — meant 2,400 (20 x 20 x 6)

three bars and two dots over them ≡ meant 6,800 (20 x 20 x 17)

Numbers 8,000 through 159,999 needed a fourth step up. The numbers on this step were 20 times larger than numbers on the third step. So—on the *fourth* step:

a dot   ·   meant 8,000 (20 x 400 x 1)

a bar —— meant 40,000 (20 x 400 x 5)

a bar and a dot over it — meant 48,000 (20 x 400 x 6)

three bars and two dots over them ≡ meant 136,000 (20 x 400 x 17)

It was easy for the Maya to write numbers in millions. They just added higher steps.

They read their numbers from top to bottom.

The Maya used the zero when there was no number on a step. The zero took the place of the number. So—when they wrote 20, they put a zero on the first step and a dot on the second step: ⦁

When they wrote 400, they put a zero on the first step, a zero on the second step and a dot on the third step: ⦁

If you want to write 23, the way the Maya did, do this . . . Find the step on which 23 fits. It fits on step two. How many 20's in 23? One twenty and 3 left over.

Write 3 dots on the first step. • • •

Write 1 dot on the second step above the 3 dots.
• • •

This is how the Maya wrote these numbers:

196 •••• 940 •• •• 8406 • •
                                              ⊙

ABOUT THE AUTHORS AND ARTIST

Tillie S. Pine and **Joseph Levine** are co-authors of the series "Science Concepts Among Peoples of Long Ago" which includes such universally accepted books as THE INDIANS KNEW, THE PILGRIMS KNEW and THE AFRICANS KNEW. They are also the authors of the "All Around" series, which includes WEATHER ALL AROUND, TREES AND HOW WE USE THEM and MAGNETS AND HOW WE USE THEM.

Ann Grifalconi has illustrated numerous children's books, one of which—THE JAZZ MAN, written by her mother, M. H. Weik—was runner up for the 1967 Newbery Medal, and was chosen one of the "10 Best Illustrated Books of 1966" by the New York Times Book Review. She has also written and illustrated her own books. The most recent one is THE TOY TRUMPET about a boy in one of the last Maya tribes.